CUTTING WASTE, REDUCING THE DEFICIT, AND ASKING ALL TO PAY THEIR FAIR SHARE

To construct an economy that is built to last and creates good jobs that pay well for generations to come, it will take making investments in education, innovation, and infrastructure so that our entrepreneurs, scientists, and workers have the tools they need to succeed. To pay for those investments and free our economy from the burden of historic deficits and growing debt, we need to change how Washington does business, and restore responsibility for what we spend and accountability for how we spend it. For too long, Washington has spent money without identifying a way to pay for it. Indeed, the cost of the 2001 and 2003 tax cuts as well as the Medicare prescription drug benefit passed in the last administration contributed significantly to turning the surpluses of the 1990s into the record deficits of the following decade. The financial crisis and recession exacerbated our fiscal situation as revenue decreased and automatic Government outlays increased to counter the recession and cushion its impact. The result was that, upon taking office, the President faced an annual deficit of $1.3 trillion, or 9.2 percent of GDP, and a 10-year deficit of more than $8 trillion—and this figure grew even larger as the depth of the recession became clear. While the need to jumpstart our economy through the Recovery Act and other measures added to the short-term deficit, these critical measures were temporary and did not have significant deficit effects beyond the recession.

In addition, for far too long, many Government programs have been allowed to continue or to grow even when their objectives are no longer clear and they lack rigorous assessment of whether the programs are achieving the desired goals. The result has been the profusion of programs that are duplicative, ineffective, or outdated—at a significant cost to taxpayers.

Since taking office the President has worked to restore accountability and fiscal responsibility. In his first Budget, the President directly confronted the unsustainable fiscal situation he inherited by making a commitment to restoring fiscal responsibility, while recognizing that increasing the deficit in the short term was necessary to arrest the economic freefall. He signed into law pay-as-you-go (PAYGO) legislation that returned the tough but disciplined budget rules of the 1990s to Washington. The principle behind PAYGO is simple: all new, non-emergency entitlement spending and revenue losses must be offset by savings or revenue increases, with no exception for new tax cuts. And, recognizing the role that rising health care costs play in our long-term fiscal future, the President advocated for and signed into law fiscally responsible health care reform that, according to the latest analysis, will reduce our deficit by more than $1 trillion over the next two decades, as well as fully pay for all new coverage. The President also convened the bipartisan National Commission on Fiscal Responsibility and Reform (the Fiscal Commission) whose work reset the debate about further deficit reduction, and who contributed many ideas that have been included in several deficit reduction plans to date.

Finally, the President pursued significant, balanced deficit reduction throughout last year: first, in February in his 2012 Budget; then, in April in the Framework for Shared Prosperity and Shared Fiscal Responsibility that built on the Budget to identify $4 trillion in deficit reduction; and next, in July, in a similarly sized plan presented to congressional Republicans during negotiations over extending the debt ceiling this summer. Unfortunately, an unwillingness by Republicans in Congress to ask the wealthiest among us to pay their fair share through any revenue increases prevented a comprehensive deficit reduction agreement from being enacted. Instead, the President signed into law the Budget Control Act of 2011 (BCA), which established discretionary spending caps that put into effect nearly $1 trillion of discretionary spending cuts. These caps impose very tight constraints on discretionary spending, and meeting them will take difficult decisions and trade-offs. In this Budget, the President has put forward a plan to meet these caps by making tough decisions that target resources toward priorities that will not undermine our ability to build a strong economy and that asks all to shoulder their fair share.

Discretionary spending is just one small part of the Budget, and the BCA also established a congressional process to cut at least $1.2 trillion more from the deficit. In August 2011, the President sent his Plan for Economic Growth and Deficit Reduction to the Joint Select Committee on Deficit Reduction, laying out how he would pay for the American Jobs Act and cut the deficit by an additional $3 trillion over the next decade.

In order to force the Congress to act and enact at least $1.2 trillion in deficit reduction, the BCA included an automatic sequester that would cut that same amount beginning in calendar year 2013 if the Joint Select Committee on Deficit Reduction failed. By design, the sequester is not good policy and is meant to force the Congress to take action: it would lead to significant cuts to critical domestic programs such as education and research and cuts to defense programs that could undermine our national security. Yet even this strong incentive to action was not enough for Republicans in Congress to agree to ask the wealthiest Americans to pay their fair share in revenue or to close special tax loopholes for large companies; thus, no action was taken, and the sequester was triggered and will take effect in January 2013 if no action is taken.

There is time for the Congress to pass a balanced, sensible plan to meet the deficit reduction goals of the BCA. And they should act to do so since cuts of this magnitude and done in an across-the-board fashion would be devastating both to defense and non-defense programs. Already, we have reduced spending on these programs, and further cuts would lead to an erosion of services that Americans would not want and undermine our national security in a way that we cannot allow. That is why in this Budget, the President again has put forward a plan that will, together with the deficit reduction enacted last year, cut the deficit by more than $4 trillion over the next decade. This would put our Nation on the right course toward a level of deficits of below 3 percent of GDP by the end of the decade. This is not an end in and of itself; rather, bringing our deficits to this level would mean that we are no longer adding to our deficits through additional spending; that debt is falling as a share of the economy; and that the country is headed in the right direction. To do this, we need to make tough choices: cutting waste where we can, reducing spending in areas that are not critical to long-term economic growth and job creation, and asking everyone to pay their fair share. Making these choices now is critical to building our economy on a solid foundation that can deliver for the middle class for years to come.

MAKING TOUGH CHOICES TO RESTORE FISCAL DISCIPLINE

To be competitive in the 21st Century, the United States cannot be weighed down by crippling budget deficits, ineffective programs that waste tax dollars, and Government spending that lacks accountability. As we move forward with the tough choices necessary to rein in our deficits and put the country on a sustainable fiscal path, we must balance those efforts with the investments and actions required to keep the economy growing and competing with other nations. We must look for cuts while protecting our core values. The Budget maintains and makes critical investments in areas important to growth and competitiveness while broadly sharing sacrifices to reduce the deficit. The Administration proposes to:

Reduce Discretionary Spending. In August 2011, the President signed into law the BCA, which put in place a down payment toward deficit reduction and a structure to accomplish even more. The BCA included a cap on discretionary spending that would achieve approximately $1 trillion in deficit reduction over the next decade. In 2012, the Congress worked in a bipartisan way to meet the caps that were agreed to in the BCA. As we turn to 2013, the caps, in combination with the drawdown in overseas contingency operations proposed in this Budget, would bring discretionary spending to its lowest level as a share of the economy since Dwight D. Eisenhower sat in the Oval Office. These are very tight caps; indeed, it would not be possible to go further and still meet the needs of the Nation. That is why achieving these cuts in discretionary spending is not easy and will take tough choices. Many programs are cut or consolidated where possible, and in some cases, only because of the demands of the fiscal situation. The Budget makes these cuts in a way that asks all to shoulder their fair share. In areas critical to building a strong, growing economy that can create good jobs that pay well, programs are not cut, but rather frozen or given small increases. In light of the caps on discretionary spending, these increases are significant.

Cut or Consolidate Programs. Allocating budgetary resources always involves a trade-off between what one wants to do and what one can afford to do. This is exacerbated when the imperative is to limit spending in order to reduce the drag of deficits and debt on our economic growth and competitiveness. In each of his first two budgets, the President put forward more than 120 terminations, reductions, and savings totaling approximately $20 billion in each year. In 2012, the Budget proposed more than 200 terminations, reductions, and savings, totaling approximately $30 billion in savings. This year, the Administration is proposing cuts and consolidations across the Government in order to live within the caps established by the BCA. To achieve these savings, we went through the Budget carefully to identify programs that were either ineffective, duplicative, or outdated and thus needed to be cut or consolidated. Other cuts were taken in programs whose mission the Administration cares deeply about, but that had to be reduced to meet our fiscal targets. A full list of these cuts and consolidations are detailed in the Budget volume, *Cuts, Consolidations, and Savings*. Furthermore, the President is pushing for the authority for even more substantial reorganizations, streamlining and consolidations—as discussed in detail below.

Implement the New Defense Strategy. Over the past three years, we have made historic investments in our troops and their capabilities, military families, and veterans. Now, we are at an inflection point after a decade of war: American troops have left Iraq; we are undergoing a transition in Afghanistan so Afghans can assume more responsibility for their security; and we have debilitated al Qaeda's leadership, putting that terrorist network on the path to defeat. At the same time, we have to renew our economic strength here at home, which is the foundation of our strength in the world, and that includes putting our fiscal house in order. That is why the President directed the Pentagon to undertake a comprehensive strategic review to ensure our defense budget is driven by a clear strategy that reflects our national interests. The key elements of the strategy are:

- Strengthening our presence in the Asia Pacific with a continued vigilance in the Middle East.

- Investing in our critical partnerships and alliances, including NATO, which has demonstrated time and again—most recently in Libya—that it is a force multiplier.

- Having ended our military commitment in Iraq and commenced a drawdown in Afghanistan, and as we look to future threats, we will no longer size our force for prolonged, large-scale stability operations. Instead, we will field smaller forces while focusing on modernization to address emerging threats.

- Continuing to get rid of outdated Cold War-era systems so that we can invest in the capabilities we need for the future, including intelligence, surveillance and reconnaissance; counterterrorism; countering weapons of mass destruction; and the ability to operate in environments where adversaries try to deny us access.

- Keeping faith with those who serve by prioritizing efforts that focus on wounded warriors, mental health, and the well-being of military families.

With this strategy as a guide, over the 10 years beginning in 2012, the Department of Defense (DOD) will spend $487 billion less than was planned in last year's Budget. The Department will realize these savings through targeted reductions in force structure; reprioritization of key missions and the requirements that support them; and continued reforms and efficiencies in acquisition, management, and other business practices. The overall defense budget, including overseas contingency operations reductions, will be down by 5 percent from the 2012 enacted level.

Establish a Budget Cap on Overseas Contingency Operations (OCO) Spending. The Budget also reflects the Administration's efforts to constrain OCO spending in the years beyond 2013. The BCA established year-by-year caps on discretionary spending for agencies' base budgets through 2021, reducing the 10-year budget deficit by about $1 trillion. However, the BCA did not limit OCO funding. Leaving OCO funding unconstrained could allow future Administrations and Congresses to use it as a convenient vehicle to evade the fiscal discipline that the BCA caps require elsewhere in the Budget. With the end of our military presence in Iraq, and as troops continue to draw down in Afghanistan, this Budget proposes a binding cap on OCO spending as well. From 2013 through 2021, the Budget limits OCO appropriations to $450 billion. Given the need for ample flexibility in budgeting for overseas contingencies, this is a multi-year total cap, rather than a series of year-by-year caps.

Require the Financial Services Industry to Pay Back Taxpayers. The Administration is calling for a Financial Crisis Responsibility Fee on the largest financial institutions to fully compensate taxpayers for the extraordinary support they provided to the financial sector, while discouraging excessive risk-taking. The assistance given to the largest financial firms represented an extraordinary step that no one wanted to take, but one that was necessary in order to stem a deeper financial crisis and set the economy on a path to recovery. The cost associated with the excessive risk-taking by the largest financial institutions continues to ripple through the economy. Furthermore, although many of the largest financial firms have repaid the Treasury for the direct Troubled Asset Relief Program (TARP) assistance they received, the entire financial system benefitted enormously from the support that TARP provided during a period of great economic upheaval. While the expected cost of the TARP program has fallen considerably from initial estimates to approximately $68 billion in the 2013 Budget, shared responsibility requires that the largest financial firms pay back the taxpayer for the extraordinary support they received as well as to discourage excessive risk taking. The fee will be restricted to financial firms with assets over $50 billion. The Administration's Financial Crisis Responsibility Fee meets the statutory requirement contained in the TARP legislation that requires the President to propose a way for the financial sector to pay back taxpayers so that not one penny of the Government's TARP-related debt is passed on to the next generation. It would extend beyond 2022 as necessary to achieve these ends, and to offset the cost of the President's new, broad-based mortgage refinancing program which is designed to help homeowners who are still suffering as a result of the financial crisis. The structure of this fee would be consistent with principles agreed to by the G-20 Leaders and similar to fees proposed by other countries. This fee will reduce the deficit by $61 billion over the first 10 years.

Restrain Increases in Federal Civilian Worker Pay. Putting the Nation back on a sustainable fiscal path will take some tough choices and sacrifices. The men and women who serve their fellow Americans as civilian Federal workers are patriots who work for the Nation often at great personal sacrifice; they deserve our respect and gratitude. But just as families and businesses across the country are tightening their belts, so too must the Federal Government. On his first day in office, the President froze salaries for all senior political appointees at the White House. In 2010, the President eliminated bonuses for all political appointees across the Administration and last year cut back on performance awards to all other employees. Starting in 2011, the President has proposed and the Congress enacted a two-year pay freeze for all civilian Federal workers, which has saved approximately $3 billion and is projected to save more than $60 billion over the next 10 years. A permanent pay freeze is neither sustainable nor desirable. However, in light of the fiscal constraints we are under, the Administration is proposing a 0.5 percent increase in civilian pay for 2013. Compared to the baseline, this slight increase in civilian pay would free up $2 billion in 2013 and $28 billion over 10 years to fund programs and services and is one of the measures the Administration proposes to help meet the discretionary caps.

Reform Federal Civilian Worker Retirement. In order to make reasonable changes to Federal worker retirement, while maintaining the ability to attract and retain highly qualified individuals, the Administration proposes to increase the employee contribution toward accruing retirement costs by 1.2 percent over three years beginning in 2013. While Federal agency contributions for currently accruing costs of employee pensions would decline, these Federal employers would pay an additional amount toward unfunded liabilities of the retirement system that would leave total agency contributions unchanged. Under the proposed plan, the amount of the employee pension would remain unchanged. We estimate this proposal will save $27 billion over 10 years. In addition, the Administration is proposing to eliminate the FERS Annuity Supplement for new employees. Overall, these changes are not expected to have a negative impact on the Administration's ability to manage its human resources, nor inhibit the Government's ability to serve the American people.

Modernize Federal Personnel Policies. To manage the complex work agencies perform today in order to meet the needs of the American people, Federal managers and employees need a modernized personnel system that reflects the reality of the 21st Century—where agencies offer compensation that reflects market competition for employees, facilitate career-development mobility across agencies and with the private sector, address poor performers consistently and fairly, develop staff, and motivate better performance using the best evidence-based public and private sector practices. To advance this effort, the Administration recommends that the Congress establish a Commission on Federal Public Service Reform comprised of Members of Congress, representatives from the President's Labor-Management Council, members of the private sector, and academic experts. The Commission would develop recommendations on reforms to modernize Federal personnel policies and practices within fiscal constraints. Such reforms could include but would not be limited to compensation, staff development and mobility, and personnel performance and motivation.

TAKING RESPONSIBILITY FOR LONG-TERM CHALLENGES TO OUR FISCAL HEALTH

In the BCA, the President signed into law a measure that will generate approximately $1 trillion in deficit reduction over the next decade through the use of discretionary spending caps. With discretionary spending projected to reach historically low levels, we cannot go any further and meet the needs and expectations of the American people. We need to look at other parts of the budget for deficit reduction. Mandatory programs, those that are not generally appropriated on an annual basis, are an important area to find savings. In some areas, these programs have not been updated or reformed for years. In others, parochial politics has allowed waste to pile up or programs to stray from their mission. In his submission to the Joint Select Committee on Deficit Reduction, the President put forward hundreds of billions of dollars in savings over 10 years in mandatory programs as well as guidelines to generate $1.5 trillion in revenue from tax reform. While the Committee was unsuccessful in its efforts to construct a bipartisan, balanced deficit reduction plan, the President is not deterred in his commitment to this goal. With a sequester poised to take effect in January 2013 that would inflict great damage on critical domestic priorities as well as the country's national security, it is especially important that the Congress come together and pass a balanced deficit reduction plan to replace this sequester and, also, go beyond its required deficit reduction.

That is why the President's Budget includes $517 billion in mandatory savings over the next 10 years and a plan for tax reform to raise more than $1.5 trillion. The President's proposal includes plans to:

Find Savings in the Agricultural Sector. A strong agricultural sector is important to maintaining a strong rural economy. The Administration is committed to a vital, robust farm economy. In recent years, we have had that: for the past decade farm income has been high and continues to increase, with net farm income forecast to be $100.9 billion in 2011, up $21.8 billion (28 percent) from the 2010 forecast—the second highest inflation-adjusted value for net farm income recorded in more than 35 years. The top five earnings years for the past three decades have occurred since 2004, attesting to the profitability of farming this decade. The Administration remains committed to a strong safety net for farmers, one that protects them from revenue losses that result from low yields or price declines, and strong crop insurance programs. But there are programs and places where current support is unnecessary or too generous. To reduce the deficit, the Administration proposes to eliminate or reduce those programs, while strengthening the safety net for those that need it most. The Administration is proposing to:

- *Eliminate Direct Payments to Farmers.* The direct payment program provides producers fixed annual income support payments for having historically planted crops that were supported by Government programs, regardless of whether the farmer is currently producing those crops—or producing any crop, for that matter. Direct payments do not vary with prices, yields, or producers' farm incomes. As a result, taxpayers continue to foot the bill for these payments to farmers who are experiencing record yields and prices; more than 50 percent of direct payments go to farmers with more than $100,000 in annual income. Eliminating these payments would save the Government roughly $23 billion over 10 years and build a better farm safety net.

- *Reduce Crop Insurance Subsidies.* Crop insurance is a foundation of our farm safety net. Yet, the program continues to be highly subsidized and costs the Government approximately $10 billion a year to run: $3 billion per year for the private insurance companies to administer and underwrite the program and $7 billion per year in premium subsidy to the farmers. A U.S. Department of Agriculture commissioned study found that, when compared to other private companies, crop insurance companies' rate of return on investment (ROI) should be around 12 percent, but that it is currently expected to be 14 percent. The Administration is proposing to lower the crop insurance companies' ROI to meet the 12 percent target, saving $1.2 billion over 10 years. In addition, the current cap on administrative expenses is based on the 2010 premiums, which were among the highest ever. A more appropriate level for the cap would be based on 2006 premiums, neutralizing the spike in commodity prices over the last four years, but not harming the delivery system. The Administration, therefore, proposes setting the cap at $0.9 billion adjusted annually for inflation, which would save $2.9 billion over 10 years. Finally, the Administration proposes to price more accurately the premium for catastrophic (CAT) coverage policies, which will slightly lower the reimbursement to crop insurance companies. The premium for CAT coverage is fully subsidized for the farmer, so the farmer is not impacted by the change. This change will save $225 million over 10 years.

In addition, the Administration is proposing to reduce producers' premium subsidy by 2 basis points for all but catastrophic crop insurance, where the subsidy is greater than 50 percent. This will have little impact on producers. Most producers pay only 40 percent of the cost of their crop insurance premium on average, with the Government paying for the remainder. This cost share arrangement was implemented in 2000, when very few producers participated in the program and "ad-hoc" agricultural disaster assistance bills were passed regularly. The Congress increased the subsidy for buy-up coverage by over 50 percent at the time to encourage greater participation. With current participation rates, the deep premium subsidies are no longer needed. This proposal is expected to save $3.3 billion over 10 years.

- *Better Target Agricultural Conservation Assistance.* The Administration has championed programs that create incentives for private lands conservation and has worked to leverage these resources with those of other Federal agencies toward greater landscape-scale conservation; however, the significant increases in conservation funding (roughly 200 percent since enactment of the Farm Security and Rural Investment Act of 2002) has led to redundancies among our agricultural conservation programs. At the same time, high crop prices have both strengthened market opportunities to expand agricultural production on the Nation's farmlands and decreased producer demand for certain agricultural conservation programs. To reduce the deficit, the Administration proposes to reduce conservation funding by $1.8 billion over 10 years by better targeting conservation funding to the most cost-effective and environmentally-beneficial programs and practices. Even under this proposal, conservation assistance is projected to grow by $60 billion over the next decade (assuming continuation of the current farm bill baseline).

Better Align Federal Worker and Military Retirement Programs. The men and women who serve their fellow Americans in the Armed Forces and civil service are patriots who work for the Nation often at great personal sacrifice. Just as families and businesses must tighten their belts to live within their means, so must the Federal Government. In addition to the proposed changes to civilian retirement noted above, one area to examine is the retirement and health benefits offered to the Federal military workforce—a group of benefits that has grown comparatively more generous than those offered in the private sector. The Administration is proposing a set of reforms to align these retirement programs better with the private sector, while still preserving the Federal Government's ability to recruit and retain the personnel that the American people need, including an adequately skilled and appropriately sized military force. The reductions sought in these retirement reforms are evenly split between civilian and military retirement programs. For military retirement reforms, the Administration proposes to:

- *Increase TRICARE Prime Enrollment Fees, Initiate Standard/Extra Annual Enrollment Fees, and Adjust Deductible and Catastrophic Caps.* DOD has implemented a variety of efficiencies within its medical program and continues to seek cost savings, but with increases in users, increased utilization, and expansion of benefits, defense health costs keep growing. In 2012, DOD implemented minor TRICARE Prime fee increases for new retiree enrollees. In 2013, DOD will phase in additional fee increases based on annual retirement pay and initiate Standard and Extra enrollment fees. Deductibles will be slightly increased and the current catastrophic cap adjusted. The Administration's proposal is estimated to save $12.1 billion in discretionary funds over 10 years.

- *Initiate Annual Fees for TRICARE-For-Life Enrollment (TFL).* Upon turning 65, military retirees and their families transition to Medicare coverage, with TFL becoming second payer. In the private sector, this type of "Medigap" policy would likely require premiums, deductibles, and copays. In 2009 the average annual premium for a Medigap policy was $2,100. By contrast, there are no premiums under the TFL programs. The Administration is proposing to introduce modest annual fees for the TFL program, based on retirement pay. This proposal is estimated to save approximately $5.9 billion in mandatory funds and $5.0 billion in discretionary funds over 10 years.

- *Make Targeted Increases to TRICARE Pharmacy Benefit Copayments.* Copayments for military members have lagged behind other Federal and private plans' copayments for prescription drugs. In an effort to slow the growth in DOD's health care costs, the President's 2012 Budget included minor pharmacy copay adjustments—which were supported by Congress. The new proposal would encourage the use of less expensive mail order and military treatment facility pharmacies. This option would have no impact on active duty members, but would affect active duty families and all military retirees regardless of the age of the beneficiary. The Administration's proposal is estimated to save $10.6 billion in mandatory funds and $17.4 billion in discretionary funds over 10 years.

- *Establish a Military Retirement Modernization Commission.* To recommend improvements to the military retirement system, the Administration is proposing to establish a Military Retirement Modernization Commission. Under the proposal, the President would appoint the Commissioners; DOD would transmit to the Commission initial recommendations to change the military retirement system; the Commission would hold hearings, make final recommendations, and draft legislation to implement its recommendations; the President would review and decide whether to transmit the Commission's

recommendations to the Congress; and Congress would vote "up or down" on the legislation. The Administration believes that any major military retirement reforms should include grandfathering provisions for current retirees and those currently serving in the military.

Reform the Aviation Passenger Security Fee to Reflect the Costs of Aviation Security More Accurately. Reflecting its commitment to keeping air travel and commerce safe, the Administration has invested heavily in personnel, technology, and infrastructure to mitigate the constantly-evolving risks to aviation security. As risk changes, however, so too must the way in which we fund our aviation security efforts. In 2001, the Aviation and Transportation Security Act created the Aviation Passenger Security Fee, which originally intended to recover the full costs of aviation security. Since its establishment, however, the fee has been statutorily limited to $2.50 per passenger enplanement with a maximum fee of $5.00 per one-way trip. This recovers only 43 percent of the Transportation Security Administration's aviation security costs, which have risen over the years while the fee has remained the same. The Administration proposes to replace the current "per-enplanement" fee structure with a "per one-way trip" fee structure so that passengers pay the fee only one time when travelling to their destination; remove the current statutory fee limit and replace it with a statutory fee minimum of $5.00, with annual incremental increases of 50 cents from 2014 to 2018, resulting in a fee of $7.50 in 2018 and thereafter; and allow the Secretary of Homeland Security to adjust the fee (to an amount equal to or greater than the new statutory fee minimum) through regulation when necessary. The proposed fee would collect an estimated $9 billion in additional fee revenue over five years, and $25.5 billion over 10 years. Of this amount, $18 billion will be deposited into the General Fund for debt reduction.

Share Payments More Equitably for Air Traffic Services. All flights that use controlled air space require a similar level of air traffic services. However, commercial and general aviation can pay very different aviation fees for those same air traffic services. To reduce the deficit and more equitably share the cost of air traffic services across the aviation user community, the Administration proposes to create a $100 per flight fee, payable to the Federal Aviation Administration, by aviation operators who fly in controlled airspace. All piston aircraft, military aircraft, public aircraft, air ambulances, aircraft operating outside of controlled airspace, and Canada-to-Canada flights would be exempted. This fee would generate an estimated $7.4 billion over 10 years. Assuming the enactment of the fee, total charges collected from aviation users would finance roughly three-fourths of airport investments and air traffic control system costs.

Provide Postal Service Financial Relief and Undertake Reform. The Administration recognizes the enormous value of the U.S. Postal Service (USPS) to the Nation's commerce and communications, as well as the urgent need for reform to ensure its future viability. USPS faces long-term, structural operating challenges that have been exacerbated by the precipitous drop in mail volume in the last few years due to the economic crisis and the continuing shift toward electronic communication. Bold action is needed to ensure that USPS can continue to operate in the short-run and achieve viability in the long-run. To that end, the President is proposing a comprehensive reform package that would: 1) restructure Retiree Health Benefit pre-funding in order to accelerate moving these Postal payments to an accruing cost basis and reduce near-year Postal payments; 2) provide USPS with a refund over two years of the $10.9 billion positive credit balance in Postal contributions to the FERS program; 3) reduce USPS operating costs by giving USPS authority, which it has said it will exercise, to reduce mail delivery from six days to five days starting in 2013; 4) allow USPS to increase collaboration with State and local governments; and 5) give USPS the ability to better align the costs of postage with the costs of mail delivery while still operating within the current price cap, and permit USPS to seek the balance of the modest one-time increase in postage rates it proposed in 2010. These reforms would provide USPS with over $25 billion in cash relief over the next two years and in total would produce savings of $25 billion over 11 years.

Strengthen the Safety Net for Workers' Retirement Benefits. All Americans deserve a secure retirement. The Administration has proposed to create new opportunities to save for retirement by establishing a system of automatic workplace pensions and doubling the small employer pension plan start-up credit. In addition, the Administration has issued regulations that would increase 401(k) fee disclosure, so that businesses can better differentiate among retirement products and workers can make more informed choices about how to invest their retirement savings. The Pension Benefit Guaranty Corporation (PBGC), which protects the retirement security of 44 million workers in defined benefit pension plans, is also critical to the success of a robust pension system. When underfunded plans terminate, PBGC assumes responsibility for paying the insured benefits. PBGC is responsible for paying current and future retirement benefits to more than 1.5 million workers and retirees. PBGC receives no taxpayer financing and relies primarily on premiums paid by insured plans. PBGC premiums are currently much lower than what a private financial institution would charge for insuring the same risk and are insufficient for PBGC to meet its long-term obligations. As of the end of September 2011, PBGC faced a $26 billion deficit. The Administration proposes to encourage companies to fully fund their pension benefits and ensure PBGC's continued financial soundness by giving the PBGC Board the authority to adjust premiums to better account for the risk the agency is insuring. This proposal consists of two parts: a gradual increase in the single-employer flat-rate premium that will raise approximately $4 billion by 2022; and PBGC Board discretion to increase the single-employer variable-rate premium to raise $12 billion by 2022. This proposal would save $16 billion over the next decade.

Restore the Solvency and Financial Integrity of the Unemployment Insurance System by Helping Employers Now and Restoring State Fiscal Responsibility. Unemployment

Insurance (UI) provides a vital safety net for workers who are laid off. Over the past several years, UI benefits have kept many families afloat during tough financial times, and in 2010 these benefits prevented 3.2 million individuals—including nearly 1 million children—from falling into poverty. UI has among the highest "bang-for-the-buck" of any measure the Federal Government could take to support near-term economic growth—generating up to $2 of economic activity for every $1 spent. The President has strongly supported expanding this critical safety net and has called for an extension of unemployment benefits for another year, along with key reforms that would help connect long-term unemployed Americans with work.

At the same time, the combination of chronically underfunded reserves and the economic downturn has placed a considerable financial strain on States' UI operations. Currently, 28 States owe more than $37 billion to the Federal UI trust fund. As a result, employers in those States are now facing automatic Federal tax increases, and many States have little prospect of paying these loans back in the foreseeable future. State UI programs also have large improper payment rates—12 percent in fiscal year 2011. The Administration proposes to put the UI system back on the path to solvency and financial integrity by providing immediate relief to employers to encourage job creation now, reestablishing State fiscal responsibility going forward, and working closely with States to eliminate improper payments. Under this Budget proposal, employers in indebted States would receive tax relief for two years. To encourage State solvency, the proposal would also raise the minimum level of wages subject to unemployment taxes in 2015 to a level slightly lower in real terms than it was in 1983, after President Reagan signed into law the last wage base increase. The higher wage base will be offset by lower tax rates to avoid a Federal tax increase. Further, the Administration has taken a number of steps to address program integrity in States that have consistently failed to place enough emphasis on combating improper payments in their UI programs. The Administration's aggressive actions have given States a number of tools to prevent improper payments, and reducing State UI error rates remains an Administration priority.

Reform Abandoned Mine Lands (AML) Payments. The coal industry as a whole is currently held responsible for cleaning up abandoned coal mines by paying a fee that finances grants to States and Tribes for reclamation. This linkage was lost, however, when the Congress in 2006 authorized additional unrestricted payments to certain States and Tribes that had already completed their coal mine reclamation work. In addition, regular reclamation funds are not well targeted at the highest priority abandoned mine lands, because amounts are distributed by a production-based formula so that funding goes to the States with the most coal production, not the greatest reclamation needs. States can use their funding for a variety of purposes, including the reclamation of abandoned hardrock mines, for which there is no other source of Federal funding. The Administration proposes to reform the coal AML program to reduce unnecessary spending and ensure that the Nation's highest priority sites are reclaimed. First, the Administration proposes to terminate unrestricted payments to the States and Tribes that have been certified for completing their coal reclamation work, since these payments do not contribute to reclaiming abandoned coal mines. Second, the Administration proposes to reform the distribution process for the remaining funds to allocate available resources competitively to the highest priority coal AML sites. Through a competitive grant program, a new AML Advisory Council will review and rank the abandoned mine lands sites, so that the Department of the Interior, in coordination with States and Tribes, can distribute grants to reclaim the highest priority coal sites each year.

Mining for hardrock minerals (e.g., silver and gold) has also left a legacy of abandoned mines across the United States. The Administration proposes to create a parallel AML program for abandoned hardrock sites. Like the coal program, hardrock reclamation would be financed by a new AML fee on the production of hardrock minerals on both public and private lands. This would hold the hardrock mining industry responsible for cleaning up the hazards left by its predecessors. The funds would be distributed through a competitive grant program to reclaim the highest priority hardrock sites on Federal, State, tribal, and private lands. Altogether, this proposal will save $1.6 billion over the next 10 years. Equally important, it would focus available coal fees to better address the Nation's most dangerous abandoned coal mines and establish a new approach to cleaning up abandoned hardrock mines across the country.

Provide a Better Return to Taxpayers from Mineral Development. The public received about $10 billion in 2011 from fees, royalties, and other payments related to oil, gas, coal, and other mineral development on Federal lands and waters. A number of recent studies by the Government Accountability Office and the Department of the Interior's Inspector General have found that taxpayers could earn a better return through more rigorous oversight and policy changes, such as charging appropriate fees and reforming how royalties are set. The Budget proposes a number of actions to receive a fair return from the continued development of these vital U.S. mineral resources: charging a royalty on select hardrock minerals (such as silver, gold, and copper); extending net receipt sharing, where States with mineral revenue payments help defray the costs of managing the mineral leases that generate the revenue; charging user fees to oil companies for processing oil and gas drilling permits and inspecting operations on Federal lands and waters, which complement new and rigorous safety and environmental standards to make sure that these activities are done responsibly; establishing fees for new non-producing oil and gas leases (both onshore and offshore) to encourage more timely production; and making administrative changes to Federal oil and gas royalties, such as adjusting royalty rates and terminating the royalty-in-kind program. Together, these changes are expected to generate approximately $3 billion in savings over 10 years.

Health Savings

Health care comprises one-quarter of non-interest Federal spending, and is the major driver of future deficit growth. To help control these costs, the President signed into law the Patient Protection and Affordable Care Act (ACA) which, according to the Congressional Budget Office's latest analysis, will reduce the deficit by more than $1 trillion over the next two decades. Realizing this deficit reduction and efficiencies in the health care system that will reduce cost and improve quality will require effective implementation of the ACA, and the President is resolutely committed to implementing ACA fairly, efficiently, and swiftly. Repealing or failing to implement health care reform would return the Nation to a path of rapidly increasing health care costs, and add trillions to deficits over the long run. The President is putting forward $364 billion in health savings that build on the ACA to strengthen Medicare, Medicaid, and other health programs by reducing wasteful spending and erroneous payments, and supporting reforms that boost the quality of care. It accomplishes this in a way that does not shift significant risks onto the individuals they serve; slash benefits; or undermine the fundamental compact they represent to our Nation's seniors, people with disabilities, and low-income families. Included are savings that would:

Reduce Medicare Coverage of Bad Debts. Today, for most eligible provider types, Medicare generally reimburses 70 percent of bad debts resulting from beneficiaries' non-payment of deductibles and copayments after providers have made reasonable efforts to collect the unpaid amounts. Similar to a proposal made by the National Commission on Fiscal Responsibility and Reform (Fiscal Commission), the Budget proposes to align Medicare policy more closely with private sector standards by reducing bad debt payments to 25 percent for all eligible providers over three years starting in 2013. This proposal will save approximately $36 billion over 10 years.

Better Align Graduate Medical Education Payments With Patient Care Costs. Medicare compensates teaching hospitals for the indirect costs stemming from inefficiencies created from residents "learning by doing." The Medicare Payment Advisory Commission (MedPAC) has determined that these Indirect Medical Education (IME) add-on payments are significantly greater than the additional patient care costs that teaching hospitals experience, and the Fiscal Commission, among others, recommended reducing the IME adjustment. This proposal would reduce the IME adjustment by 10 percent beginning in 2014, and save approximately $10 billion over 10 years.

Better Align Payments to Rural Providers With the Cost of Care. Medicare makes a number of special payments to account for the unique challenges of delivering medical care to beneficiaries in rural areas. These payments continue to be important; however, in specific cases, the adjustments may be greater than necessary to ensure continued access to care. The Administration proposes to improve the consistency of payments across rural hospital types, provide incentives for efficient delivery of care, and eliminate higher than necessary reimbursement. To improve payment accuracy for Critical Access Hospitals (CAHs), the Administration proposes to reduce payments from 101 percent to 100 percent of reasonable costs, effective in 2013, and to eliminate the CAH designation for those that are fewer than 10 miles from the nearest hospital, effective in 2014. These changes will ensure that this unique payment system is better targeted to hospitals meeting the eligibility criteria and will save approximately $2 billion over 10 years.

Encourage Efficient Post-Acute Care. Medicare covers services in skilled nursing facilities (SNFs), long-term care hospitals (LTCHs), inpatient rehabilitation facilities (IRFs) and home health. Over the years, expenditures for post-acute care have increased dramatically, and payments in excess of the costs of providing high quality and efficient care place a drain on Medicare. Recognizing the importance of these services, the Administration supports policies that will save approximately $63 billion over 10 years and

improve the quality of care. These include adjusting payment updates for certain post-acute care providers, equalizing payments for certain conditions commonly treated in IRFs and SNFs; encouraging appropriate use of inpatient rehabilitation hospitals; and adjusting SNF payments to reduce unnecessary hospital readmissions.

Align Medicare Drug Payment Policies With Medicaid Policies for Low-Income Beneficiaries. Under current law, drug manufacturers are required to pay specified rebates for drugs dispensed to Medicaid beneficiaries. In contrast, Medicare Part D plan sponsors negotiate with manufacturers to obtain plan-specific rebates at unspecified levels. The Department of Health and Human Services' Inspector General has found substantial differences in rebate amounts and net prices paid for brand name drugs under the two programs, with Medicare receiving significantly lower rebates and paying higher prices than Medicaid. Moreover, Medicare per capita spending in Part D is growing significantly faster than that in Parts A or B under current law. This proposal would allow Medicare to benefit from the same rebates that Medicaid receives for brand name and generic drugs provided to beneficiaries who receive the Part D Low-Income Subsidy beginning 2013. Manufacturers previously paid Medicaid rebates for drugs provided to the dual eligible population prior to the establishment of Medicare Part D. The Fiscal Commission recommended a similar proposal to apply Medicaid rebates to dual eligibles for outpatient drugs covered under Part D. This proposal is estimated to save $156 billion over 10 years.

Increase Income-Related Premiums Under Medicare Parts B and D. Under Medicare Parts B and D, certain beneficiaries pay higher premiums as a result of their higher levels of income. Beginning in 2017, the Administration proposes to increase income-related premiums under Medicare Parts B and D by 15 percent and maintain the income thresholds associated with income-related premiums until 25 percent of beneficiaries under Parts B and D are subject to these premiums. This will help improve the financial stability of the Medicare program by reducing the Federal subsidy of Medicare costs for those beneficiaries who can most afford them. This proposal will save approximately $28 billion over 10 years.

Modify Part B Deductible for New Beneficiaries. Beneficiaries who are enrolled in Medicare Part B are required to pay an annual deductible. This deductible helps to share responsibility for payment of Medicare services between Medicare and beneficiaries. To strengthen program financing and encourage beneficiaries to seek high-value health care services, the Administration proposes to apply a $25 increase in the Part B deductible in 2017, 2019, and 2021 for new beneficiaries. Current beneficiaries or near retirees would not be subject to the revised deductible. This proposal will save approximately $2 billion over 10 years.

Introduce Home Health Copayments for New Beneficiaries. Medicare beneficiaries currently do not make copayments for Medicare home health services. This proposal would create a home health copayment of $100 per home health episode, applicable for episodes with five or more visits not preceded by a hospital or other inpatient post-acute care stay. This would apply to new beneficiaries beginning in 2017. This proposal is consistent with a MedPAC recommendation to establish a per episode copayment. MedPAC noted that "beneficiaries without a prior hospitalization account for a rising share of episodes" and that "adding beneficiary cost sharing for home health care could be an additional measure to encourage appropriate use of home health services." This proposal will save approximately $350 million over 10 years.

Introduce a Part B Premium Surcharge for New Beneficiaries That Purchase Near First-Dollar Medigap Coverage. Medigap policies sold by private insurance companies provide beneficiaries additional support for covering healthcare costs by covering most or all of the cost sharing Medicare requires. This protection, however, gives individuals less incentive to consider the costs of health care services and thus raises Medicare costs and Part B premiums. Of

particular concern are Medigap plans that cover substantially all Medicare copayments, including even the modest copayments for routine care that most beneficiaries can afford to pay out of pocket. To encourage more efficient health care choices, the Administration proposes a Part B premium surcharge equivalent to about 15 percent of the average Medigap premium (or about 30 percent of the Part B premium) for new beneficiaries that purchase Medigap policies with particularly low cost-sharing requirements, starting in 2017. Current beneficiaries and near-retirees would not be subject to the surcharge. Other Medigap plans would be exempt from this requirement while still providing beneficiaries options for protection against high out-of-pocket costs. This proposal will save approximately $2.5 billion over 10 years.

Strengthen the Independent Payment Advisory Board (IPAB) to Reduce Long-Term Drivers of Medicare Cost Growth. Created by the ACA, IPAB has been highlighted by economists and health policy experts as a key contributor to Medicare's long term solvency. Under current law, if the projected Medicare per capita growth rate exceeds a predetermined target growth rate, IPAB recommends to the Congress policies to reduce the rate of Medicare growth to meet the target. IPAB recommendations are prohibited from increasing beneficiary premiums or cost-sharing, or restricting benefits. To further moderate the rate of Medicare growth, this proposal would lower the target rate from the GDP per capita growth rate plus 1 percent to plus 0.5 percent. Additionally, the proposal would give IPAB additional tools like the ability to consider value-based benefit design.

Cut Waste, Fraud, and Abuse in Medicare and Medicaid. In this fiscal environment, we cannot tolerate waste, fraud, and abuse in Medicare, Medicaid, and the Children's Health Insurance Program (CHIP)—or any Government program. That is why the Administration has introduced its Campaign to Cut Waste, together with long-standing efforts to boost program integrity and reduce improper payments (that is, payments made to the wrong person, in the wrong amount, or for the wrong reason).

The Administration is aggressively implementing the new tools for fraud prevention included in the ACA. Also, it is implementing the fraud prevention system, a predictive analytic model similar to those used by private sector experts. In addition, the Administration is proposing a series of policies to build on these ongoing efforts that will save nearly $5 billion over the next 10 years. Specifically, the Administration proposes to: create new initiatives to reduce improper payments in Medicare; dedicate penalties for failure to use electronic health records toward deficit reduction; update Medicare payments to more appropriately account for utilization of advanced imaging; require prior authorization for advanced imaging; direct States to track high prescribers and utilizers of prescription drugs in Medicaid to identify aberrant billing and prescribing patterns; and affirm Medicaid's position as a payer of last resort by removing exceptions to the requirement that State Medicaid agencies reject medical claims when another entity is legally liable to pay the claim. Additionally, the Budget would alleviate State program integrity reporting requirements by consolidating redundant error rate measurement programs to create a streamlined audit program with meaningful outcomes, while maintaining the Federal and State's government ability to identify and address improper Medicaid payments.

Phase Down the Medicaid Provider Tax Threshold Beginning in 2015. Many States impose taxes on health care providers to help finance the State share of Medicaid program costs. However, some States use those tax revenues to increase payments to those same providers and use that additional spending to increase their Federal Medicaid matching payments. The Administration proposes to limit these types of State financing practices that increase Federal Medicaid spending by phasing down the Medicaid provider tax threshold from the current law level of 6 percent in 2014, to 4.5 percent in 2015, 4 percent in 2016, and 3.5 percent in 2017 and beyond. By delaying the effective date until 2015, the proposal gives States more time to plan for the change. This proposal is projected to save $21.8 billion over 10 years.

Apply a Single Blended Matching Rate to Medicaid and CHIP Starting in 2017. Under current law, States face a patchwork of different Federal payment contributions for individuals eligible for Medicaid and CHIP. Specifically, State Medicaid expenditures are generally matched by the Federal Government using the Federal medical assistance percentage (FMAP); CHIP expenditures are matched with enhanced FMAP (eFMAP); and the ACA provides increased match for newly-eligible individuals and certain childless adults beginning in 2014. This proposal would replace these complicated formulas with a single matching rate specific to each State that automatically increases if a recession forces enrollment and State costs to rise beginning in 2017. This proposal is projected to save $17.9 billion over 10 years.

Limit Medicaid Reimbursement of Durable Medical Equipment (DME) Based on Medicare Rates. Under current law, States have experienced the same challenges in preventing overpayments for DME that previously confronted Medicare. The Medicare program is in the process of implementing innovative ways to increase efficiency for payment of DME through the DME Competitive Bidding Program, which is expected to save the Medicare program more than $25 billion and Medicare beneficiaries approximately $17 billion over 10 years. This proposal extends some of these efficiencies to Medicaid, starting in 2013, by limiting Federal reimbursement for a State's Medicaid spending on certain DME services to what Medicare would have paid in the same State for the same services. This proposal is projected to save $3.0 billion over 10 years.

Re-Base Medicaid Disproportionate Share Hospital (DSH) Allotments in 2021 and Beyond. This proposal continues the ACA policy to better align Medicaid DSH payments with reductions in the number of uninsured in 2021 and beyond. Supplemental DSH payments are intended to help support hospitals that provide care to disproportionate numbers of low-income and uninsured individuals. The ACA reduced State DSH allotments by $18.1 billion through 2020 to reflect the reduced need as a result of the increased coverage provided in the Act. The Administration proposes to compute 2021 State DSH allotments based on States' actual 2020 DSH allotments, better aligning future Medicaid supplemental payments to hospitals with reduced levels of uncompensated care. This proposal is projected to save $8.3 billion over 10 years.

Expand State Flexibility to Tailor Benefit Packages to Meet the Needs of Beneficiaries. This proposal would give States flexibility to require "benchmark" benefit plan coverage for non-elderly, non-disabled adults with incomes over 133 percent of the Federal poverty level. Currently, States have the option to provide certain populations "benchmark" or "benchmark equivalent" plans, or alternative benefit packages that may be offered in lieu of the benefits covered under a traditional Medicaid State plan.

Prohibit "Pay for Delay" Agreements to Increase the Availability of Generic Drugs and Biologics. The high cost of prescription drugs places a significant burden on Americans today, causing many to skip doses, split pills, or forgo needed medications altogether. The Administration proposes to increase the availability of generic drugs and biologics by authorizing the Federal Trade Commission to stop companies from entering into anti-competitive deals, known also as "pay for delay" agreements, intended to block consumer access to safe and effective generics. Such deals can cost consumers billions of dollars because generic drugs are typically priced significantly less than their branded counterparts. These agreements reduce competition and raise the cost of care for patients both directly, through higher drug and biologic prices, and indirectly through higher health care premiums. The Administration's proposal facilitates greater access to lower-cost generics and will generate $11 billion over 10 years in savings to Federal health programs including Medicare and Medicaid.

Modify the Length of Exclusivity to Facilitate Faster Development of Generic Biologics. Access to affordable lifesaving medicines is essential to improving the quality and efficiency of health care. The Administration's proposal ac-celerates access to affordable generic biologics by modifying the length of exclusivity on brand name biologics. Beginning in 2013, this proposal would award brand biologic manufacturers seven years of exclusivity rather than 12 years under current law and prohibit additional periods of exclusivity for brand biologics due to minor changes in product formulations, a practice often referred to as "evergreening." Reducing the exclusivity period increases the availability of generic biologics by encouraging faster development of generic biologics while retaining appropriate incentives for research and development for the innovation of breakthrough products. The Administration's proposal strikes a balance between promoting affordable access to medications and encouraging innovation to develop needed therapies. The proposal will result in $4 billion in savings over 10 years to Federal health programs including Medicare and Medicaid.

Tax Reform

The President is committed to reducing the deficit through a balanced approach—one that restrains spending across the Budget, including in the tax code; asks the wealthiest among us to contribute to deficit reduction; and lays the foundation for future growth. That is why the President is calling on the Congress to undertake comprehensive tax reform to cut rates, cut inefficient tax breaks, cut the deficit, and increase jobs and growth in the United States—while observing the "Buffett Rule" that people making over $1 million should not pay lower taxes than the middle class.

Tax reform is critical to rebuilding our economy to be stronger and more stable than in the past. Two of our biggest economic challenges—creating jobs and reducing long-term deficits—both depend on instituting a simpler, fairer, more progressive tax system than we have today. The Administration believes, like many others, that well-designed tax cuts can play an important role in job creation now. But the Administration believes that immediate, broad tax cuts for the middle class—rather than for only the wealthiest 1 or 2 percent of Americans—are far more effective at creating jobs and growing the economy. When millions of middle-class families across the country have more money in their bank accounts to spend in their communities, businesses large and small can grow, innovate, invest, and hire. The success of the American economy has long been built on the vibrancy of our middle class, and our efforts to create a tax system that is fairer, simpler, and more progressive reflect that reality.

Tax reform is also an important part of reducing our long-term deficits and placing our country on a fiscally sustainable path. We cannot address a deficit a decade in the making through spending cuts alone—that is, unless we, as a country, agree to cut every program in the entire budget by more than a quarter, including defense spending, Social Security payments, Medicare benefits, and veterans' benefits, along with everything else. The Administration believes in a balanced approach that cuts spending responsibly, but also asks the most well-off in society—many of whom, through loopholes and other exemptions, pay less in taxes than most middle-class families—to contribute their fair share toward reducing the deficit and invigorating our economy.

Unfortunately, the tax code has become increasingly complicated and unfair. Changes enacted during the previous Administration were skewed in favor of the wealthiest taxpayers and reduced the tax code's overall progressivity. Under today's tax laws, those who can afford expert advice can avoid paying their fair share and interests with the most connected lobbyists can get exemptions and special treatment written into our tax code. While many of the tax incentives serve important purposes, taken together the tax expenditures in the law are inefficient, unfair, duplicative, and often unnecessary. The corporate tax system provides special incentives for some industries, like oil and gas producers, yet fails to provide sufficient incentives for companies to invest in America. Because our corporate tax system is so riddled with special interest loopholes, our system has one of the highest statutory tax rates among developed countries to generate about the same amount of corporate tax revenue as our developed country

partners as a share of our economy; this, in turn, hurts our competitiveness in the world economy. In addition, a large fraction of the tax code is now temporary and expires periodically, adding uncertainty for households and businesses, and complicating the fiscal outlook.

The result is a tax code that neither serves the American people nor our economy. In September, the President announced five principles for tax reform. The President stands by those principles as elaborated upon below. Tax reform should:

- *Simplify the Tax Code and Lower Tax Rates.* The tax system should be simplified and work for all Americans with lower individual and corporate tax rates and fewer tax brackets.

- *Reform Inefficient and Unfair Tax Breaks— Eliminating Them for Millionaires While Making All Tax Breaks at Least as Good a Deal for the Middle Class as for Wealthy Americans.* Reform should cut and simplify tax breaks that are now inefficient, unfair, or both, so that wealthiest Americans cannot avoid their responsibilities by gaming the system, that middle class working Americans receive their fair share, and that Americans can spend less time and money each year filing taxes. That means eliminating tax subsidies for millionaires that they do not need; there is no reason that those making over $1 million should get any tax subsidies for housing, health care, retirement, and child care. And it means ensuring fair incentives for the middle class to buy a home or save for retirement, as opposed to allowing the most well-off to get two to three times as much.

- *Decrease the Deficit While Protecting Progressivity.* Reform should cut the deficit by $1.5 trillion over the next decade through tax reform, including the expiration of tax cuts for single taxpayers making over $200,000 and married couples making over $250,000. And it should do this while keeping the tax code at least as progressive as if the high-income

2001 and 2003 tax cuts were eliminated, as the President proposes.

- *Increase Job Creation and Growth in the United States.* The tax code should make America stronger at home and more competitive globally by increasing the incentive to work and invest in the United States. This includes fundamental corporate tax reform. That is why, in addition to these principles, the President is proposing a roadmap for corporate tax reform that will make America more competitive and create jobs here at home.

- *Observe the Buffett Rule.* No household making over $1 million annually should pay a smaller share of its income in taxes than middle-class families pay. As Warren Buffett has pointed out, his effective tax rate is lower than his secretary's. And, the President is now specifically proposing that in observance of the Buffett rule, those making over $1 million should pay no less than 30 percent of their income in taxes. The Administration will work to ensure that this rule is implemented in a way that is equitable, including not disadvantaging individuals who make large charitable contributions. And he is proposing that the Buffett rule should replace the Alternative Minimum Tax, which now burdens middle-class Americans rather than stopping the richest Americans from paying too little as was originally intended.

This will make our tax code simpler, fairer, and more efficient—and end a system that allows households making millions of dollars annually to pay lower tax rates than middle-class families.

To begin the national conversation about tax reform, the President is offering a detailed set of specific tax loophole closers and measures to broaden the tax base that, together with the expiration of the high-income tax cuts, would be more than sufficient to hit his $1.5 trillion target for tax reform, pay for tax cuts for the middle class, cut inefficient expenditures, and move the tax system closer to observing the Buffett rule. Included are measures that would:

Allow the 2001 and 2003 High-Income Tax Cuts to Expire and Return the Estate Tax to 2009 Parameters. The tax cuts for those with household income above $250,000 per year passed in the Bush Administration were unfair and unaffordable at the time they were enacted and remain so today. In December 2010, congressional Republicans insisted on extending them through 2012 and threatened to allow taxes to increase on middle-class families if the Administration did not agree. Not extending the middle-class tax cuts would have hurt our nascent economic recovery, and would have imposed an enormous burden on working families; as a result, the Administration agreed to extend them to 2012 as part of a deal that also included immediate support for the economy in the form of a payroll tax cut and an extension of unemployment insurance. The Administration remains opposed to the extension of these high-income tax cuts past 2012 and supports the return of the estate tax exemption and rates to 2009 levels. This would reduce the deficit by $968 billion over 10 years.

Reduce the Value of Itemized Deductions and Other Tax Preferences to 28 Percent for Families With Incomes Over $250,000. Currently, a millionaire who contributes to charity or deducts a dollar of mortgage interest, enjoys a deduction that is more than twice as generous as that for a middle-class family. The proposal would limit the tax rate at which high-income taxpayers can reduce their tax liability to a maximum of 28 percent, affecting only married taxpayers filing a joint return with income over $250,000 (at 2009 levels) and single taxpayers with income over $200,000. This limit would apply to: all itemized deductions; foreign excluded income; tax-exempt interest; employer sponsored health insurance; retirement contributions; and selected above-the-line deductions. The proposed limitation would return the deduction rate to the level it was at the end of the Reagan Administration. It would reduce the deficit by $584 billion over 10 years.

Tax Carried (Profits) Interests as Ordinary Income. Currently, many hedge fund managers, private equity partners, and other managers in partnerships are able to pay a 15 percent capital gains rate on their labor income (on income that is known as "carried interest"). This tax loophole is inappropriate and allows these financial managers to pay a lower tax rate on their income than other workers. The President proposes to eliminate the loophole for managers in investment services partnerships and to tax carried interest at ordinary income rates. This would reduce the deficit by $13 billion over 10 years.

Eliminate Special Depreciation Rules for Corporate Purchases of Aircraft. Under current law, airplanes used in commercial and contract carrying of passengers and freight can be depreciated over seven years. Airplanes not used in commercial or contract carrying of passengers or freight, for example corporate jets, are depreciated over five years. The proposal would change depreciation schedules for corporate planes that carry passengers to seven years to be consistent with the treatment of commercial aircraft. This would reduce the deficit by $2 billion over 10 years.

Eliminate Oil and Gas Tax Preferences. The tax code currently subsidizes oil and gas production through loopholes and tax expenditures that preference these industries over others. Current law provides a number of credits and deductions that are targeted toward certain oil and gas activities. In accordance with the President's agreement at the G-20 Summit in Pittsburgh in December 2009 to phase out subsidies for fossil fuels so that we can transition to a 21st Century energy economy, the President is proposing to repeal a number of tax preferences available for fossil fuels. Getting rid of these would reduce the deficit by $41 billion over 10 years.

CREATING A GOVERNMENT THAT IS EFFECTIVE AND EFFICIENT

Whether the Budget is in surplus or deficit, wasting taxpayer dollars on programs that are outdated, ineffective, or duplicative is wrong. With the tight discretionary caps implemented by the BCA, we have no choice but to redouble our efforts to scour the Budget for waste and to make tough decisions about reducing funding or ending programs that are laudable, but cannot be funded in this fiscal environment. This exercise is difficult, but builds on the efforts the Administration has undertaken since the President took office. As part of its Campaign to Cut Waste, the Administration has moved to cut wasteful spending and programs that do not work, strengthen and streamline what does work, leverage technology to transform Government operations to save money and improve performance, and make Government more open and responsive to the needs of the American people. As the President said in his 2011 State of the Union address, we cannot win the future with the government of the past. In order to win the future and better serve a more competitive America, we need a 21st Century government that is efficient, effective and accountable. To continue these efforts, the Administration proposes to:

Reorganize Government. We live and do business in the information age, but the organization of our Government has not kept pace, changing little since the days of black and white TV. Over the years, duplicative efforts sprang up that made it less effective, wasting taxpayer dollars, and making it harder for the American people to navigate their Government. To create an economy that is built to last, will take a private sector that has at its disposal all it needs to compete with firms and workers from around the world. That means re-organizing government so that it does more for less, and that it is best positioned to assist businesses and entrepreneurs grow and win in the world economy. That is why the President has asked the Congress to revive an authority that Presidents had for almost the entire period from 1932 through 1984: to submit proposals to reorganize the Executive Branch via a fast-track procedure. The Administration's proposal, the "Reforming and Consolidating Government Act of 2012," would enable the President to submit plans to consolidate and reorganize Executive Branch departments and agencies for fast track consideration by the Congress, but only so long as the result would be to reduce the size of Government or cut costs, the latter being a new requirement for this type of authority.

If given this authority, the President would submit a proposal to consolidate a number of agencies and programs into a new Department with a focused mission to foster economic growth and spur job creation. The proposal would consolidate the six primary business and trade agencies, as well as other related programs, integrating into one new Department the Government's core trade and competitiveness functions. Specifically, the new Department will absorb the Department of Commerce's core business and trade functions, the Small Business Administration, the Office of the U.S. Trade Representative, the Export-Import Bank, the Overseas Private Investment Corporation, and the U.S. Trade and Development Agency. It will also incorporate related programs from a number of other departments, including the Department of Agriculture's business development programs, the Department of the Treasury's Community Development Financial Institutions Fund program, the National Science Foundation's statistical agency and industry partnership programs, and the Bureau of Labor Statistics from the Department of Labor. Creating a department with a laser-focus on economic growth requires moving the National Oceanic and Atmospheric Administration to the Department of the Interior.

By bringing together the core tools to expand trade and investment, grow small businesses, and support innovation, the new Department could coordinate these resources to maximize the benefits for businesses and the economy. With more effectively aligned and deployed trade promotion resources, strengthened trade enforcement capacity, streamlined export finance programs, and enhanced focus on investment in the United States, the Government could better implement a strong, pro-growth trade policy. This reorganization would help American businesses compete more effectively in the global economy, expand exports, and create more jobs at home. Businesses will more easily and seamlessly be able to access services in support of exports, domestic competi-

tiveness, and job creation. The Administration expects these changes to generate approximately $1.5 billion in savings over the next 10 years by reducing overhead and consolidating offices and support functions, as well as additional, comparable savings through programmatic cuts once the synergies from consolidation are realized, for a total of $3 billion over the next 10 years.

Cut Improper Payments by $50 Billion. Each year, the Federal Government wastes billions of American taxpayers' dollars on improper payments to individuals, organizations, and contractors. These are payments made in the wrong amount, to the wrong person, or for the wrong reason. In the summer of 2010, the President set a goal of cutting improper payments by $50 billion between 2010 and 2012. The Administration is on track to meet or exceed this goal, having avoided more than $20 billion in improper payments in 2010 and 2011 combined. In 2011, the Government-wide improper payment rate declined to 4.69 percent, a sharp decrease from the 5.29 percent reported in 2010. Agencies also reported that they recaptured more than $1.2 billion in overpayments to contractors and vendors in 2011. This was the highest recapture amount reported in the eight years that agencies have reported results. In total, the Federal Government has recaptured $1.9 billion in 2010 and 2011 combined, and the Administration is less than $100 million away from meeting the President's goal to recapture $2 billion by the end of 2012.

Dispose of Excess or Under-Utilized Federal Property. With over 1.1 million buildings, structures, and land parcels, the Federal Government is the largest property owner and manager in the country. In 2010, agencies identified tens of thousands of excess and underutilized real property assets (both civilian and military assets) that represent hundreds of millions of taxpayer dollars spent annually on unnecessary operation and maintenance costs, as well as other opportunities for reforming the inventory that could create billions of dollars in savings through streamlined efficiencies and reduced operating costs. In June 2010, the President directed agencies to accelerate efforts to shed unneeded property and reduce operating costs in order to achieve $3 billion in non-defense savings by the end of 2012. To date, Federal agencies have achieved $1.5 billion in savings and identified enough savings opportunities to exceed the $3 billion goal for non-defense savings opportunities. In addition, the DOD has achieved roughly half of its $5 billion goal for Base Realignment and Closure (BRAC) related savings.

Despite these successes, there is bipartisan agreement that competing stakeholder interests and red tape continue to significantly hinder the disposal of Government property. There remain numerous high-value assets within the civilian real estate inventory that are no longer needed to support Federal agency missions and represent unnecessary costs to the taxpayer. Faced with similar challenges, DOD utilized BRAC, a streamlined process, to dispose of military properties and achieve billions of dollars of savings over the last 20 years. Building off the best practices of BRAC, the Administration proposed the Civilian Property Realignment Act (CPRA) in the 2012 Budget. The proposal would create an independent Board of experts to identify opportunities to consolidate, reduce, and realign the Federal footprint as well as expedite the disposal of properties. This proposal utilizes bundled recommendations, a fast-track congressional procedure, streamlined disposal and consolidation authorities, and a revolving fund replenished by proceeds to provide logistical and financial support to agencies, as a comprehensive solution to the key obstacles that prevent the Federal Government from effectively managing its real estate, and could make a significant contribution to deficit reduction. The Administration will continue to aggressively pursue the CPRA in 2013 so the Federal Government can cut through red tape and competing stakeholder interests to more quickly dispose and consolidate civilian properties and realize billions of dollars in savings for taxpayers.

Reduce Administrative Overhead. In his very first Cabinet meeting, the President asked his Cabinet to find at least $100 million in collective cuts to their administrative budgets, separate and apart from those identified in the Budget. They responded by identifying 77 cost-saving measures, amounting to $243 million in savings through 2010. Continuing that effort, the 2012 Budget included agency-specific, targeted cuts to administrative expenses such as travel, printing, supplies, and advisory contract services. The total administrative savings is estimated to be over $2 billion. Building upon that effort, the President issued an Executive Order to promote efficient spending in November 2011. The Executive Order called for agencies to make a 20 percent reduction in their spending on the administrative areas targeted in the 2012 Budget, as well as three additional areas: employee information technology devices, extraneous promotional items, and executive transportation. Overall, this will yield nearly $8 billion in savings in 2013 compared to 2010 spending on these administrative activities, which agencies are redirecting to higher priority programs.

Save Billions of Dollars in Contracting. The President's mandate to improve Federal procurement practices has stopped uncontrolled contract spending and put agencies on a path for achieving real and sustained improvement. After over a decade of dramatic increases in contract spending, contracting decreased in 2010 for the first time in 13 years—with agencies spending $80 billion less than what they would have, if contract costs had continued to grow at the same rate as they did from 2000 to 2008. In 2011, agencies maintained this lower level of spending by buying less, ending contracts that were unaffordable or no longer needed, improving the workforce's ability to negotiate better deals and hold contractors to their promise of delivering on time and on budget, and reducing the use of high-risk contracts, including time-and-materials contracts, where agencies reimburse contractors for the hours they work instead of the results they achieve. Agencies also increased their use of Government-wide contracts to leverage the Federal Government's buying power as the world's largest customer, saving taxpayers tens of millions of dollars for everyday needs, like office supplies and overnight delivery services.

In 2012, the Administration will continue its efforts to deliver better value to taxpayers. Agencies will reduce by 15 percent spending on management support service contracts, where contract spending has far outpaced the already fast growth in contracting generally and one that has been prone to risk, including the risk of overreliance on contractors. Agencies will also strengthen their suspension and debarment programs to better ensure that bad actors who put taxpayer dollars at risk of waste, fraud, and abuse are prohibited from doing work with Federal agencies. In addition, they will continue to build the capabilities of the acquisition workforce, by improving training and developing specialized cadres to better manage information technology procurements as well as centers of excellence to facilitate the rapid adoption of best practices for achieving stronger program outcomes.

Reform Military Acquisition. DOD contracts account for approximately 70 percent of all Federal procurement. Through its "Better Buying Power" acquisition reform initiative, DOD is charting a new path that will result in greater efficiency and productivity throughout the defense acquisition system. In particular, DOD is: 1) decreasing the use of high-risk contracts based on time-and-materials and labor-hours; 2) continuing to develop the acquisition workforce to provide needed oversight; 3) eliminating or restructuring lower-priority acquisitions; 4) reducing contract spending on management support services; 5) taking full advantage of contract vehicles that reflect the Government's buying leverage; 6) increasing the use of strategic sourcing; 7) increasing small business participation; and 8) improving financial management systems. In addition, DOD has instituted a number of acquisition management best practices: applying lessons learned from past acquisitions; establishing process teams to review qualifications of acquisition professionals; and instituting peer reviews to ensure affordability and effective competition. In a world of tight discretionary budget caps, these reforms will help free up resources that can be devoted to higher-priority programs.

Reduce Energy Costs for the Federal Government's Biggest Consumer. DOD consumes almost three-fourths of all Federal energy resources. To reduce consumption, the Budget includes approximately $1 billion for energy conservation investments at DOD—up from $400 million in 2010. These investments include making energy retrofits of existing buildings, meeting energy efficiency standards in new buildings, and developing renewable energy projects. DOD is steadily improving its installation energy performance by reducing the demand for traditional energy and by increasing the supply of renewable energy, currently 8.5 percent of DOD energy production and procurement. The request includes $150 million for the Energy Conservation Investment Program, which improves the energy efficiency of DOD facilities worldwide. In addition, the Budget provides $32 million, a 7 percent increase compared to 2012, for the Installation Energy Test Bed Program to demonstrate new energy technologies to reduce risk, overcome barriers to deployment, and facilitate wide-scale commercialization.

Harness Information Technology to Do More with Less. The American people expect the Government to use information technology (IT) to provide the same level of service they experience in their everyday lives. As part of the Accountable Government Initiative, the Administration is transforming how the Government uses IT to improve productivity, lower the cost of operations, and streamline service delivery, all while bolstering cyber security. By taking a hard look at Government IT projects through Tech-Stats, over the last three years we have avoided project costs of nearly $4 billion—while also accelerating the time it takes to get usable products up and running. To reduce duplicative spending, the Administration has already shut down over 140 Government data centers and is on track to close nearly 1,100 by the end of 2015. Overall, the data center optimization efforts are expected to yield $3 to $5 billion in savings. And through the "Cloud First" policy, agencies are shifting from a capital-intensive model toward a more flexible operational model where they pay only for the services they use. The ultimate goal is to improve service to the American people. To do this, we must lower the barriers to interaction with the Government. That is why the Administration launched a one-stop, online portal for small businesses to find and access available programs, information, and other services from across the Government rather than having to waste time navigating the Federal bureaucracy. Going forward, the Administration will continue to harness the transformational power of IT to build the Government of the 21st Century and to help agencies deliver more effectively on their missions. By doing more with less, the Administration is driving savings across Government and using those savings to reinvest in information technology and services that benefit the American people.

The Federal Government is also improving how it acquires IT products and services through the use of early vendor engagement in complex and high-risk IT procurements and the development of specialized IT acquisition cadres that increase the chance of successful program outcomes.

Reduce Outdated and Duplicative Reporting. While the plans and reports that Congress requires of the Executive Branch often serve legislative decision-making, oversight and public transparency, they can become outdated, duplicative, or less useful than when originally mandated. Under the GPRA Modernization Act, the Congress instructed the Executive Branch to identify outdated or redundant reports to consolidate, streamline, or eliminate. Agencies identified more than 9,000 plans or reports currently produced for the Congress, with DOD responsible for approximately 70 percent of them. Of these, agencies proposed more than 450 low-priority plans and reports for the Congress to consider eliminating or consolidating. These reports currently take Federal employees approximately 200,000 hours to prepare and result in almost 30,000 pages. Concurrent with the Budget, the list of plans and reports identified for possible elimination or consolidation have been posted for public comment on *Performance.gov*. After collecting public comments, OMB will work with the Congress to eliminate or consolidate plans and reports that have become outdated or duplicative.

Adopt Performance-Based Reforms. Widely viewed as leveraging more change than any other competitive grant program in history, the Department of Education's Race to the Top (RTT) initiative spurred States across the Nation to bring together teachers, school leaders, and policymakers to achieve difficult yet fundamental improvements to our education system. By setting out clear standards that needed to be met to receive funds, RTT instigated change in States all across the Nation, including even those that ultimately did not receive RTT funds. By doing so, RTT has driven taxpayer dollars to be used more effectively. The RTT approach is being expanded to transform and improve lifelong learning from early childhood education through college and beyond; to allocate grants for transportation; to bring innovation to workforce training; and to accelerate advanced vehicle deployment.

Improve Outcomes with Better Evidence. In order to understand what works and what does not in the Federal Government, and thus better use taxpayer dollars, rigorous evaluations of results are critical. Agencies must establish a culture where they constantly ask, and try to answer, questions that help them find, implement, spread, and sustain effective programs and practices; find and fix or eliminate ineffective ones; test promising programs and practices to see if they are effective and can be replicated; and find lower-cost ways to achieve a positive impact. The Federal fiscal situation necessitates doing more with less, not only to reduce budget deficits, but to build confidence that Americans are receiving maximum value for their hard-earned tax dollars. It is therefore critical to apply an evidence-based approach to government management that utilizes rigorous methods appropriate to the situation, learns from experience, and is open to experimentation. Agencies are conducting evaluations across the Federal Government, and the Recovery Act launched a number of evaluations that are currently underway on such topics as the effects of different rent formulas on housing assistance recipients, the effects of electricity pricing treatments in combination with advanced metering infrastructure (including smart meters) on residential electricity usage, and the effects of extended unemployment insurance benefit programs on employment outcomes. In addition, the Administration is placing additional focus on agency evaluation budgets to ensure that those dollars are producing high quality evidence that informs key decisions.

Use Goals and Frequent Data-Driven Reviews to Achieve More Results for the Money. In these fiscal times, it is it more important than ever for Government agencies to use taxpayer money wisely to achieve greater program impact for the taxpayer's dollar. A careful review of past experience shows that government works better when leaders identify a limited number of clear, measurable, and ambitious goals and regularly review progress toward them. Building on these lessons from two prior years, senior agency leaders identified with their 2013 budget submissions a limited number of near-term Agency Priority Goals (formerly called High Priority Performance Goals) that require neither additional resources nor legislative action, but rather hinge on strong execution to be accomplished. They have also designated a senior accountable official, a "Goal Leader," responsible for driving progress on each goal. For the first time, as part of the 2013 Budget process, the Administration has also set a limited number of agency Federal Cross-Agency Priority Goals in areas where increased cross-agency coordination or learning, regular review, and designation of a goal leader are expected to accelerate progress. Agency and Cross-Agency 2013 Priority Goals have been set in a wide variety of areas. Some focus on increasing U.S. exports, broadband coverage, entrepreneurship opportunities, and the science and technology workforce. Others focus on reducing the cost of clean energy technologies, such as advanced vehicles and improving the energy efficiency of the Nation's homes and industries while reducing costs for families. Some seek to improve the well-being of the Nation's children and adults, especially veterans who served the Nation so well, while others seek to prevent bad things, such as fatalities and health-care associated infections, from happening and reduce their costs when they do. Several goals seek to cut the costs of delivery, while sustaining high quality customer service.

Pay for Success in Domestic Programs. Many traditional Government social programs fit one of two molds: prescriptive programs that stifle innovation by specifying eligible providers and activities, or flexible block grants that fail to focus on results. To ensure taxpayers get the best possible return on their investment, the Administration is testing a new program model—Pay for Success—in which the Government provides flexibility for how services are delivered and pays for results after they are achieved. The working capital for a Pay for Success project generally comes from private investors that bear the risk of failure, but receive a financial return if the project succeeds. Projects use and build evidence-based practices to improve the lives of vulnerable target populations, reducing their need for future Government services and cash assistance. Over the course of 2012, the Administration is launching a small number of Pay for Success pilots in criminal justice and workforce development. The President's 2013 Budget reserves a total of up to $109 million to test this new financing mechanism in a broader range of areas including education and homelessness. If successful, Pay for Success projects offer a cost-effective way to replicate effective practices and support continuing innovation as Federal resources become more constrained.

Empower Local Communities to Achieve Better Results. Inconsistent and overlapping Federal program requirements sometimes prevent States and localities from effectively coordinating services or using funding to support strategies that are likely to achieve the best outcomes. This is especially true for cross-cutting policy areas, such as disconnected youth and distressed neighborhoods, where multiple programs, each with its own requirements, all contribute to the same broad goals. Performance Partnership pilots provide a model for enabling leading edge States and localities to demonstrate better ways to use resources, by giving them flexibility to pool discretionary funds across multiple Federal programs in exchange for greater accountability for results. In 2013, the Administration proposes to establish a limited number of Performance Partnership pilots designed to improve outcomes for disconnected youth or to support the revitalization of distressed neighborhoods. All affected Federal agencies and the Director of the Office of Management and Budget would have to approve of the agreement and confirm that vulnerable populations would not be adversely affected, before a Performance Partnership pilot could be established.